# THE ORDINARY AFFAIR OF BEING HUMAN

**TIMI SANNI**

*For those who have gone, and for what remains human in us*

Published by Akashic Books

ISBN: 978-1-63614-252-4


Printed in China
First printing

EU Authorized Representative details:
Easy Access System Europe
Mustamäe tee 50, 10621 Tallinn, Estonia
gpsr.request@easproject.com

Akashic Books
Instagram, X, Facebook: AkashicBooks
info@akashicbooks.com
www.akashicbooks.com

African Poetry Book Fund
Brown University
10 Prospect Street
Box A
Providence, RI 02912

# TABLE OF CONTENTS

## PREFACE

*by Gbenga Adesina*

Think of a psalm of fragility, an emotional archive of those who are broken and those who do the breaking, and how sometimes both are pods of the same startled seeds, and you might arrive at Timi Sanni's *The Ordinary Affair of Being Human*, a talismanic chapbook of poems curated against death. The poems are kinetic by design and prescient in their diagnosis of a family's malady, their intimacy with death. The family is not a metaphor, and yet it *is* a metaphor—for a nation. In that context, the poems, scored with an ear toward an economy of rhythm, invite us into a young poet's narrative logic as he weighs a spiritual conflict: his simultaneous inheritance of fragility and brutality.

A surrealistic investigation of the entropic Nigerian reality undergirds these twelve finely attuned poems. Sanni has rightly intuited that myths are often able to illuminate what is obscure in a lineage, nation, and society. He invites the reader to ponder a fable in which a knife in the hand of a boy becomes the blood of an animal which stains his spirit as he carries that stain from city to city, heaven to heaven, guilty of the sins of his father and brothers. A parable for trammeled innocence—or perhaps there was never innocence, only guilt waiting to ripen. Guilt may be passed down through generations like a genetic code. Here, citizens are inheritors of their society's legacy of violence, spiritual famine, and drought of affection. He wrestles with this.

In the poem "Origin Story," a seven-stanza lyrical memoir told in episodic vignettes, Sanni traces a moral trajectory that begins with a boy's tender kinship with vulnerable animals, his desire to protect them and recognize them as equals in the family of living beings. However, the arc ends painfully, with the boy's initiation into the atmospheric cult of trampling upon the weak: "Once, I watched my dad kill . . ." The poet asks us to consider the boy's subsequent transmogrification into a hand capable of inducing death.

In the following poem, "Crisis," this metaphor of fragility and transmogrification takes on an even more ominous dimension as it shifts its gaze to a vulnerable infant. Sanni recounts a nearly fatal medical crisis, an agitated mother cradling a child to her chest, and a father angry and envious at being usurped in the domestic hierarchy of affection. But Sanni is not interested in sentimentality; his project is a surrealistic fable, a mirror in which we might see ourselves. Hence, in the same poem, he questions a world in which the vulnerable only command attention through their proximity to death. He blurs the line between child and father, destabilizing our notions of the victim and villain, lest we traffic in settled interpretations.

Throughout *The Ordinary Affair of Being Human,* these themes—oscillation of personas, interspecies relations, and kinship with animals as equal possessors of sentience, hunger, and destinies, coupled with the language of interiority—lend potency to Sanni's myths and stories. Ultimately, we are invited to read this chapbook of poems as a talisman against death: death hovers, haunts, and lusts after the presences in this book, but Sanni refuses to concede ground. Even in the poem "If You Could Trick Death with a Name"—which brings to mind Ben Okri's *The Famished Road* and Ayobami Adebayo's *Stay With Me*—though the subject is *abiku,* a spirit child in Yoruba cosmology that repeatedly dies and is reborn, never reaching maturation, Sanni's focus is the mother's whispered plea for a language that blinds death.

Whether in a poem like "Bàtá," where history, art, and language are tools to investigate a society's psyche; or "Litany," a finely wrought psalm for fragile things; or "The Tradition," a particularly musical and liturgical elegy that recalls the incantatory genius of Nome Emeka Patrick; or "The Origin of Sweetness," the poet demonstrates a musical facility, lyrical impulse, and narrative technique. Sanni has an instinct for distilled histories, and by letting his poems seep past the borders of the private into the discursive, he lends his voice and project credence.

# WORMHOLE

This is the season where grace is most difficult;
hunger, prominent; the body constantly running
out of fuel. Hey, wild hands drumming,
can I have that boyish zeal? Windows clapping,
red dogs barking in the streets, can I have again
those gone days where the only consequence
was *fun*? I am losing the heart of my youth. I am
stacking, with shaky hands, jagged rocks
by the shore of this blue dream—knowing
that every pebble is a moment balanced in time,
and waiting for the collapse. How now the wind
tears through it all. This is not how it ends. This
must not be how it ends. Tell me about that year
when I threaded the eye of a storm, how life
had only just begun, how it was cold and no one
could breathe. I was on a mare, somewhere
in the sky, and all around me the clouds were falling,
cotton fluff by cotton fluff by cotton fluff, when
at once, I pierced the fabric of the world and sewed shut
the mouth of the rogue wind. I can do it all again.

# *PART ONE: ORIGIN*

## ORIGIN STORY

*after Tara Bray's "Memoir"*

Once, I watched my dad kill a hen we'd reared for years;
watched my brother carry its small, limp body. *Why?*
I cried. *Her neck is bleeding now*. Everyone laughed.
I refused to eat its meat. I could not fathom the betrayal.

At school, a boy loved his sheep so much that once
when he called home to ask about them, he jumped up
all of a sudden, screaming, *Twins! Twins!* We all thought
his mom had put to bed. But it was just his pregnant ewe.

Once, my cousins named their goat Champion,
and it grew up to be that—stubborn, reckless, proud,
and so smart it knew to answer to its name. We talked
of the future, of time, of the marriage of the goat.

We were only boys with bushy hair and eyes so kind
they glowed. Ravaged and gritty as a stone, we played ball
barefoot in the sands. What we didn't know
of consequences came to break us.

The blade is a dangerous thing. I killed once
and never forgot. The pain like a wound—blood
so wrong it carries the stench of sacrilege. A body, so full
of life, and then, in time, stiff. I spent all day trying
to pray away the evidence of the knife.

Once, at a family reunion, we ducked beneath the hands
of our parents and ran, laughing, into the streets. On the ride

home, we held hands and danced, the scenery wafting past
like a slow song. We thought we could dance forever.

Now, I remember only that morning, the call,
my cousin's voice breaking as he said, "We killed
and ate Champion." Now, the silence between us
spreads thick as butter on dry bread. The oven of the mouth,
gone cold and quiet, witnesses the horror it made.

## CRISIS

As a child, small and sick, my mother
doted over me in fear—
child of promise, held to breast
even as my father, one midnight,
stormed out of the house in anger
at my mother who wouldn't
put me down, the night bleeding
long into a sorry song of vengeance.
Who wouldn't want
a story like mine—to be the bone
of contention lodged
in the fleshy meat of marriage?
I mean, don't you dream
of something greater than love—
an apothecary potent in its delight;
walking into a room and seeing
someone storm out, blistered
with envy? I won't say a thing
about regret, though it's been many
long years since that child was held.
Once, during a difficult year,
it was said, my sister held me to her
chest like a lamb as I dropped
in and out of God's light.
The body, faithful in its work,
tallies these absences like clockwork.
It is 2001 all over again. I appear
in this story as my father and see
all the love that should have been mine

doing time in a sickle cell.
The truth is not far from the wound.
The only times I have been poured
a decent measure of love
have been with my body folded over
in crisis. I love myself a little
more, if only to bear the pain.

## IF YOU COULD TRICK DEATH WITH A NAME

We watch the mother stare,
unflinching, at the death of her newborn,
and whisper, in that din of spirits,
Àbíkú, look, there is no plea left
in these eyes you worsted with tears.
Sorrow burns, old names crackle
with glee—we see Bámitálẹ̀ go up
in flames, Dúrójayé following
into the ash like a lost lamb. In this dearth
of memory, we watch the darkness
as it watches the mother
watching her newborn,
tender as the underbelly of love.
We see her spit a name so vile it stinks
and slap it on his face. Nobody
remembers when we began to cry
in our place beneath that tree
in the shadow of God, where we did not
realize that this was the hardest act
of love—the mother,
on smacking the child, signing
*please don't leave, my baby,*
hoping death, blind to this nuance,
goes off in search
of other precious things.

## BÀTÁ

I have seen men with hair the color of rust
whip caution like sand to the wind
at the sound of the bàtá drums.
In my language, the word for bee
is the same for honey, which is to say: a man
is what he makes with the machinery of his body.
Look at what we make with ours.
In truth, elixirs are only fancy words
for alchemy's sting. Observe, people of the world,
the drum and its folk, the avian rhythm by which,
again, we mistake feet for wings.
It is no fault of the drum. A goat laid down its life
for the miracle of this music, and it may be the gods'
only boon to us. Men have killed for it.
Even the white Europeans who knew nothing
of the sun to which from birth we've pledged
our skins—they came, in those dark years, and carted
away with it. Only there was no one to coax out
its fine music. No one. Not until centuries later,
when, like a god, it returned. And there we were waiting
to beat it back into its joy. In the eyes of God, my people
are a beehive stirred into passion by the
beekeeper's wanton smoke. Driven mad by duty, look
at what merry we make with the wind. How once,
during a festival, my town was raided, the huts
burned, the crops reaped, but no one
stopped dancing, because the music . . . the music.
How we filled up on melody, filled up
so much we made a home of the air.

## LITANY

*after Ernest Ògúnyẹmí's "song"*

& what was the song
of our making, our scheming
lying, waking—our stirring
& stirring the burden of the pot,
sweet, mellow brew fermenting
in the cask like an ache.
what was the song
in that forest of desire,
red petals in their wake,
branches restless,
o, what was that autumn song.
purple bird, yellow bread,
silver beard, earthen bed.
even the broth spilling
at the end of the rainbow
was not enough, nor the coins
glinting in their royal fires,
yellow ship afloat
on the grace of the sea, want
like a furious wind in its sail.
whose heart was it I heard
shattering
across the frozen lake,
whose wing was it that snapped
like a twig caught
in its stormy fate. I am doomed
to descent, as I am
doomed to flight, doomed

to love, as I am doomed to fall.
o, what am I becoming,
burnt root, bent
lute, angst's gong,
lost song, abomination,
aberration—between
the world & me, Wright wrote
and then it ended—
the line—between the world
& me. what followed
was the image of silence—o God,
not mine, this body damned
& silent.

# *PART TWO: LIGHT*

## THE TRADITION

A body touched by death loses
all forms of resistance. I know this
in the story of my grandmother
whose throat at death could hold
no morsel. At that precious hour,
between her head and body, lay
not a throat by any means,
but a small, dark tunnel, famished,
unavailing, what strength it took
to reject that which—already too late—
would do it no good; opening, instead,
like a floodgate, life, as liquid,
falling through it like muddy water
through the bleak hollow of a tap.
I will never forget the haunting
drip of the pap as it dropped
into the gourd of her belly.
It was the women's idea to force-
feed her to life. From heaven,
a manna of light descended,
illumination so intense, her body
splintered, spirit from flesh.
And suddenly, her tongue,
white with that wisdom of death,
and heavy, could not speak
the language of men.

•••

In the corner of the room, an angel sat,
its folded wings an array
of blades. Death was the operation.
The bedroom, a makeshift theater.
Everywhere smelled of mud. I forgot,
briefly, the fragrance of flowers. I felt
instead their rage. In the wind that
clapped the windows like an act,
I felt the sting of death's bite,
tiny gashes, almost imperceptible to skin.
To deliver a soul is no small feat.
What exists as the body must suffer.
Witness its brilliant labor. Where,
at genesis, did the soul know to enter?
Now, it must find that impractical exit;
rummage through the hallways of the body
till something gives. No one wants
to watch their grandmother die, exorcised
of the ghost of purpose. No one wants
to witness their grandmother, the glorious
mystery, bottomless pit of folktales,
fall back into those old stories.
But as her breath gave way to a sigh,
all I could think was the tradition
of stories, those carried from mouth
to mouth like a kiss or song, those held
to breast like a child or secret. All which,
by virtue of being, must come to an end.

## WISDOM TOOTH GROWING, OR AGAINST THE NATURE OF EMPIRES

I find it unnatural, cruel even,
that the tooth must break
the gum to crown,
as if for the sake of glory
something must bleed,
must break.
Little white soldier
in that troop of the mouth;
enameled ruin
of the little red plain,
you appear with your trademark
ache from that horizon of the body
where the rot of the empire throbs
in collision with light.
Your bayonet breaks
through defenseless flesh;
your empire crests
like a wave.
And in that critical edge, slowly,
you grow
into your "wisdom."
The tongue, like a pope, must continue
its work of diplomacy
oscillating between teeth and gum
though the damage is as linear as a blade
of grass that breaks the earth for light.
The ruin of the soil is collateral
in the plants' policy of living.

In every place I have found beauty,
I have found, also,
something in search of glory,
shedding its compassion like a coat—
like Congo, its cobalt mines tainted
with the empire's capital curse;
like the Middle Eastern lands
with their oil wells raped into blood.
I am looking away from nature,
its sacrilege of blood on ice,
from that essence of man
which concerns itself with conquest,
toward heaven, where
at least my pain is mine.
To inherit heaven, I killed no man,
I cheated no brother of mine;
I forfeited instead my living
for a life of ink and paper;
lived as a poem in defiance
of ruin. In the time of genocide,
I existed as a petition for peace.

## THE ORIGIN OF SWEETNESS

In the wild, beneath a bowed palm tree,
red-chested monkeys gather
around a pile of bananas, yellow ripe as longing,
jabbering and jabbering, bare bottoms
deep in the mud as they munch fruit
after fruit. I watch from my house of leaves.
They could leave a void in the place
of the mountain, and still cry *hunger*.
Or they could eat enough to realize
that even a giant dream would not fill
the appetite for life, that the treetops lie bare
deep in the woods, their branches aching
in their wait for the mischief of limbs.

When I failed a test at school,
I crammed my mouth full of suya
to simulate the experience of joy.
But when I swallowed, everything,
even the salt, tasted bitter in my mouth.
How long was it before I traced the origin
of sweetness to its one eternal source?
All my life, I've held an emptiness
inside me, and tried to fill it with food,
money, lust, power. It wasn't until I arrived
at hunger, like a bird flying empty
into the morning sky, that I knew
how faith kept the belly full.

I watch as, one by one, the monkeys
begin to leave, to heed the voice that calls
in the silence of the trees. I watch
as one sits there stubbornly, sole god
of the yellow dream, eating what the others
forsook, in wisdom, for meaning.

# THE ORDINARY AFFAIR OF BEING HUMAN

Tell me about pride, and I will tell you
of the humility of the wingless.
The more I saw my heroes, the more
ordinary they became—flesh as soft,

bone as brittle, blood even redder
than the crimson of marrows.
On earth, there is nothing more
extraordinary than just being human.

All that lies on the horizon of this
is vanity. The arrow that breaks
a kiwi's skin will break the falcon's.
And I have seen giant birds bleed.

It's ugly. I prefer the beauty of their lush
feathers, the tempest of their winds.
So let no bird get so drunk on the high winds
that it stares down the arrow point of death.

We'll wait for our miracle of wings; sing,
"*this body of mine will endure.*" And because
the dance is beautiful, we'll let the music
go on a little longer.

# ACKNOWLEDGMENTS

Much gratitude to the editors of the following publications where these poems first appeared:

*Agbowó Magazine:* "Wormhole"
*Cincinnati Review:* "Origin Story"
*Frontier Poetry:* "If You Could Trick Death with a Name"
*HOAX:* "The Ordinary Affair of Being Human"
*lean and loafe:* "The Origin of Sweetness"
*ONLY POEMS:* "Crisis" and "Wisdom Tooth Growing, or against the Nature of Empires"
*Poet Lore:* "litany"
*trampset:* "Bàtá"